JAPANESE FLORAL STENCIL DESIGNS

EDITED BY

JAMES SPERO

DOVER PUBLICATIONS, INC., NEW YORK

PUBLISHER'S NOTE

For centuries Japanese craftsmen have been famous for the skills they manifest in the applied arts. In particular, the textiles they have produced, ranging from the most elaborate brocades and embroideries to intricate tie-dyed and stenciled cloths, reveal their great ingenuity and acute artistic sensibilities.

Stenciled fabrics allowed members of the middle class to dress in brightly patterned clothing that had previously been limited to the ruling classes. Wooden stencils were eventually replaced by stencils made of several layers of paper that were used in the application of a rice-paste resist. The complex stencils were cut by masters who used a wide variety of blades and awls. The trade reached its peak during the Tokugawa Shogunate (1603–1868) in the city of Suzuka in the Mie Prefecture and on the island of Okinawa.

In this anthology, stencils featuring patterns based predominantly on floral and plant motifs have been selected. The subjects included are especially popular with the Japanese: iris, peony, cherry blossom, chrysanthemum, gentian, paulownia, maple leaf, pine, bamboo, honeysuckle and various grasses. These are frequently combined with images of cranes, phoenixes, waterfowl and objects such as hats, fences and bridges. The patterns are often displayed asymmetrically, but are also laid out in classic arrangements such as lozenges, *karakusa* scrolls (p. 66, top), the hemp-leaf pattern (p. 89, bottom) and the *saya* pattern (p. 93, top).

Although these stencils were designed with textiles specifically in mind, their graphic value is such that they can be used to effect in many projects that require the elegant touch that distinguishes Japanese art.

Copyright © 1991 by Dover Publications, Inc.
All rights reserved under Pan American and International Copyright Conventions.

Published in Canada by General Publishing Company, Ltd., 30 Lesmill Road, Don Mills, Toronto, Ontario.
Published in the United Kingdom by Constable and Company, Ltd., 3 The Lanchesters, 162–164 Fulham Palace Road, London W6 9ER.

Japanese Floral Stencil Designs, a new work, first published by Dover Publications, Inc., in 1991, consists of a publisher's note and a selection of designs from published Japanese sources.

DOVER *Pictorial Archive* SERIES

Manufactured in the United States of America
Dover Publications, Inc., 31 East 2nd Street, Mineola, N.Y. 11501

Library of Congress Cataloging-in-Publication Data

Japanese floral stencil designs / edited by James Spero.
    p.   cm. — (Dover pictorial archive series)
    ISBN 0-486-26655-9
    1. Decoration and ornament—Plant forms—Japan—Themes, motives. 2. Stencil work—Japan. I. Spero, James. II. Series.
NK1484.A1J37   1991
746.6—dc20
                                       90-27348
                                         CIP

1

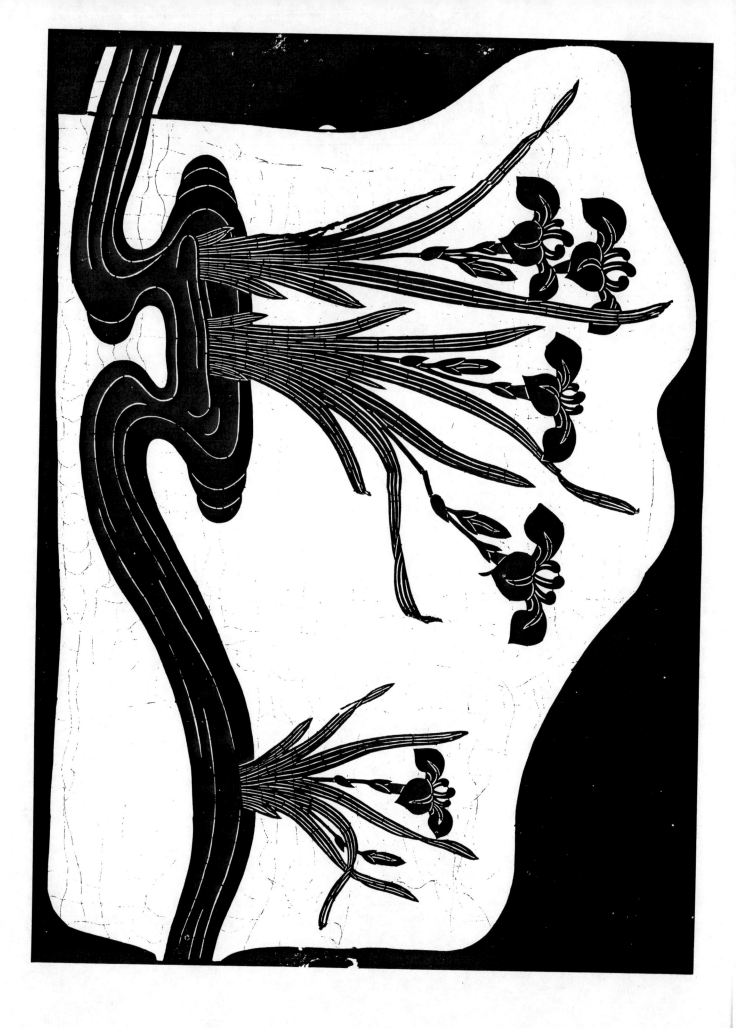

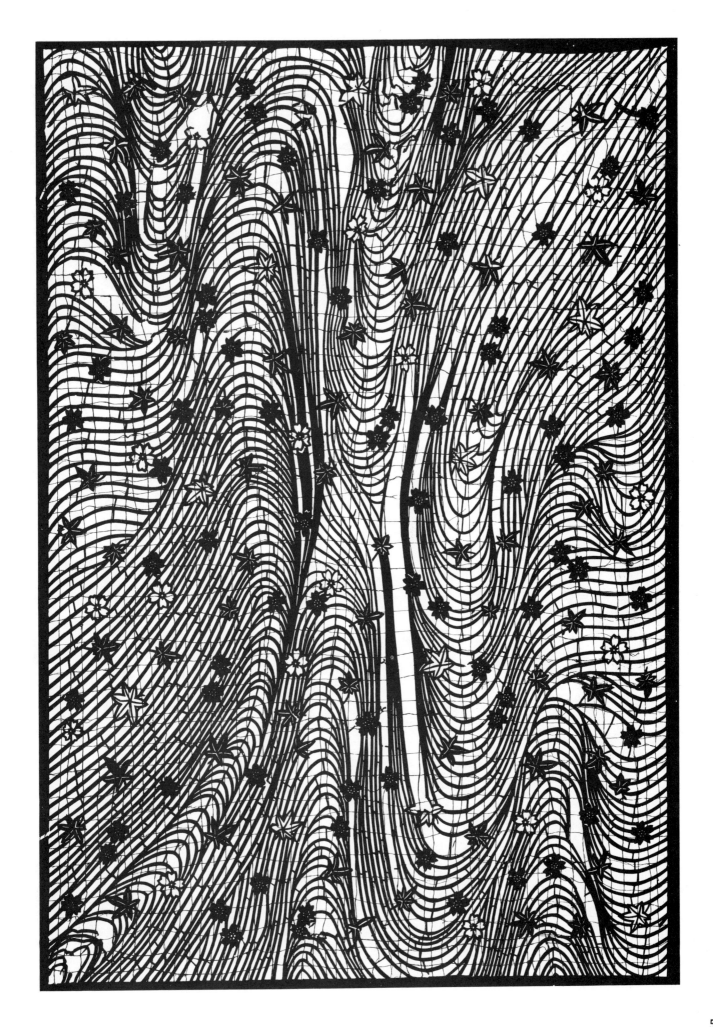

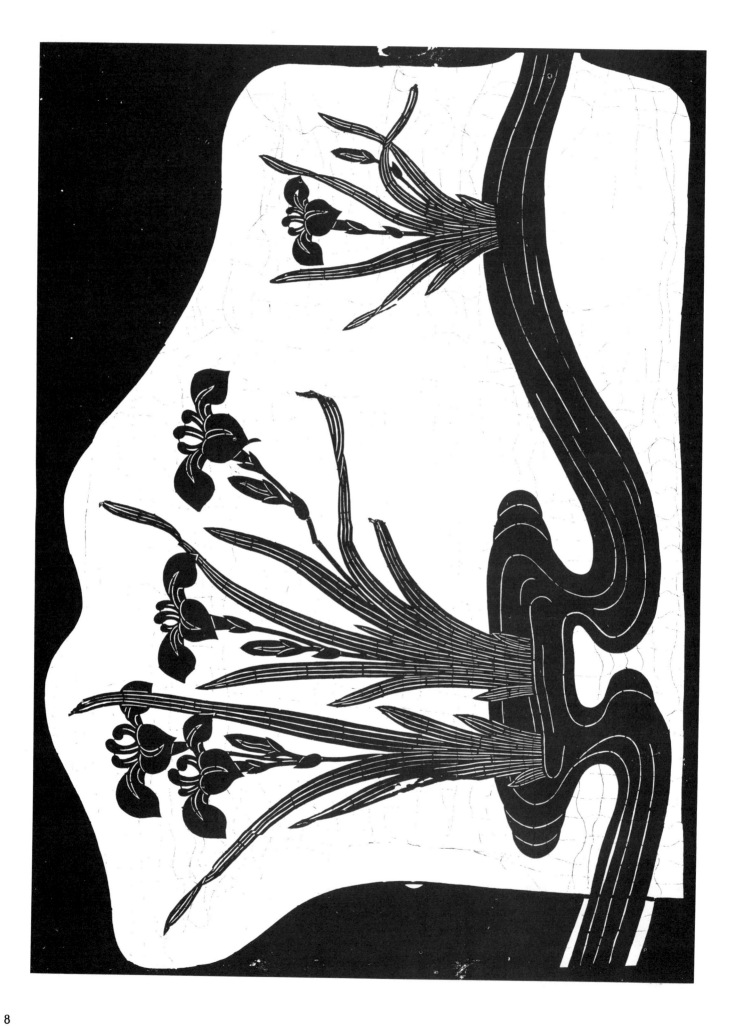

8

10

12

24

28

38

43

53

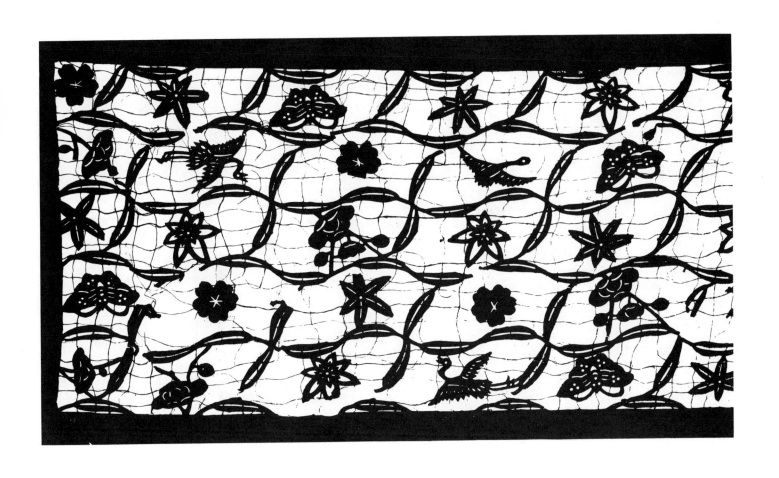

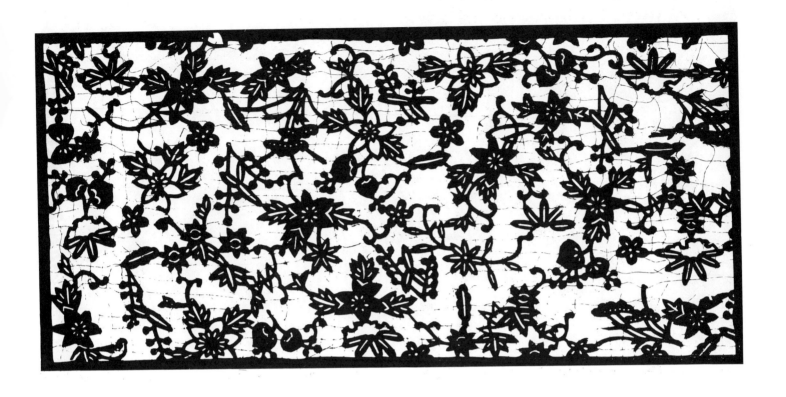

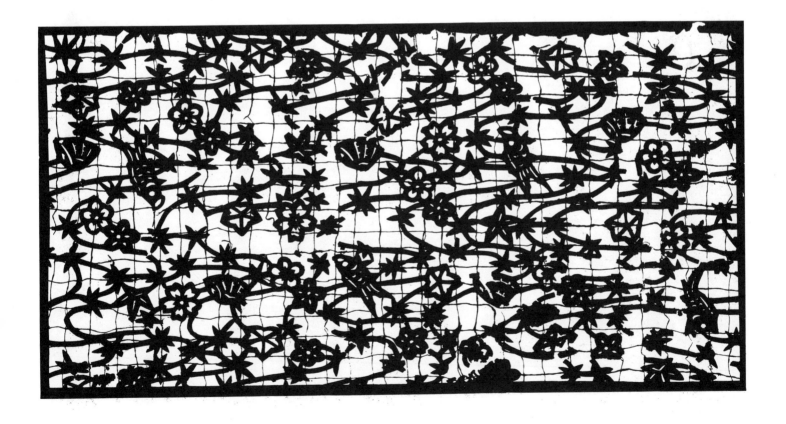

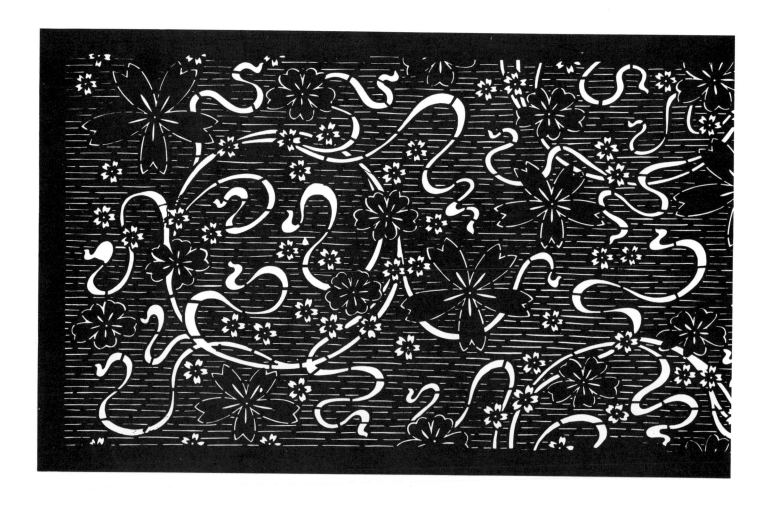

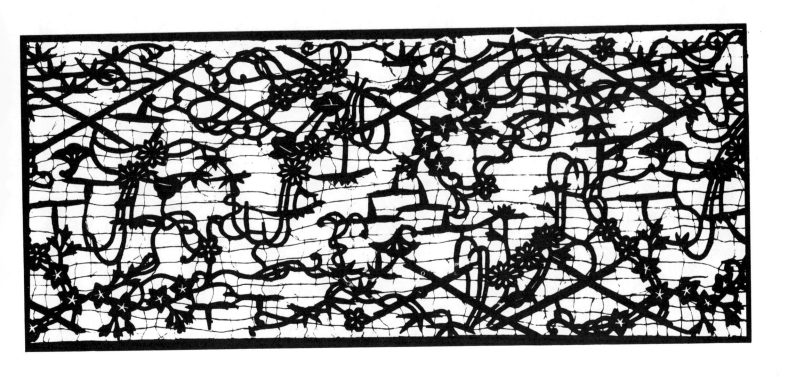

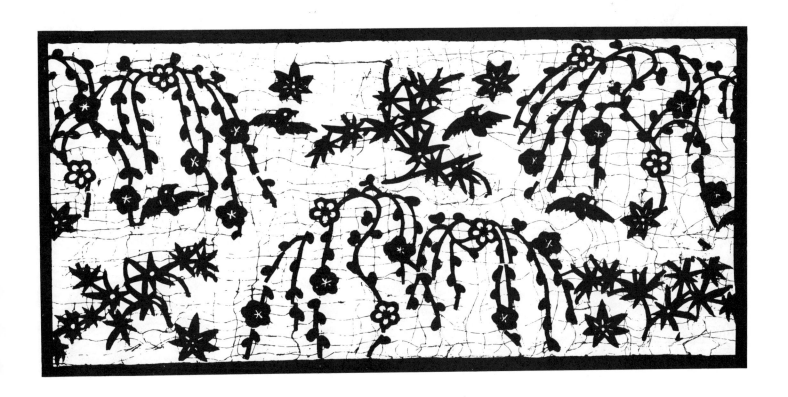

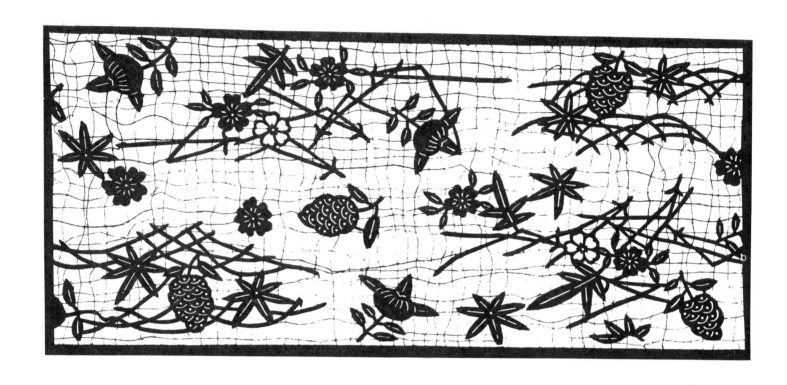

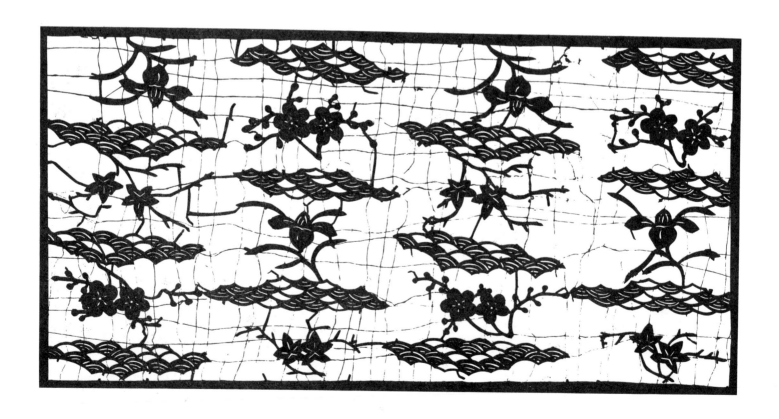

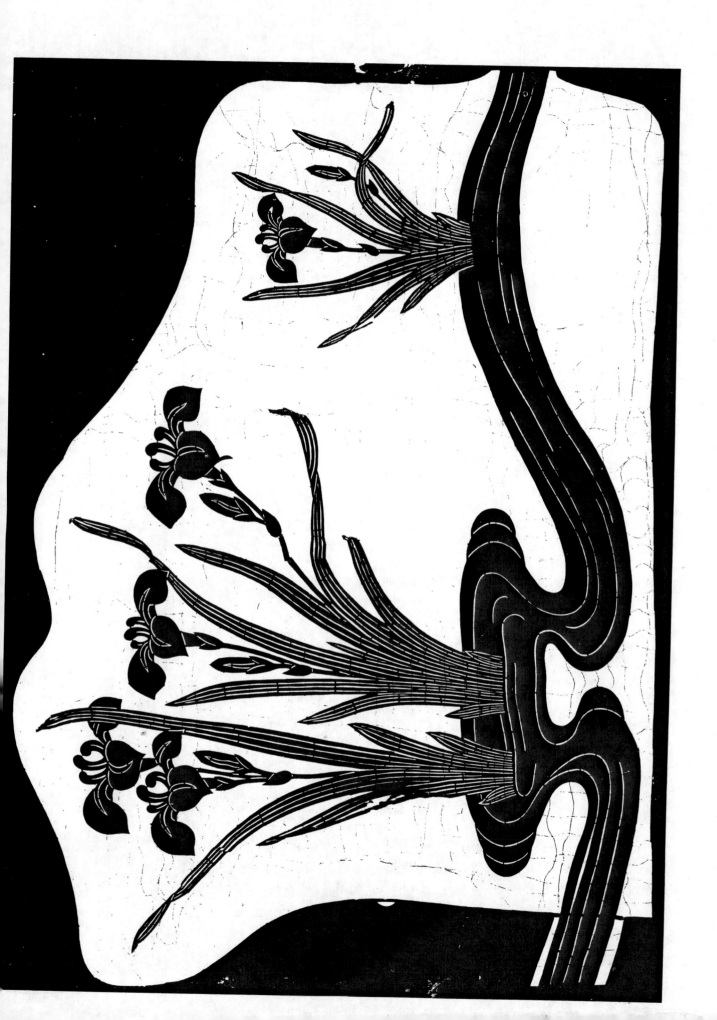

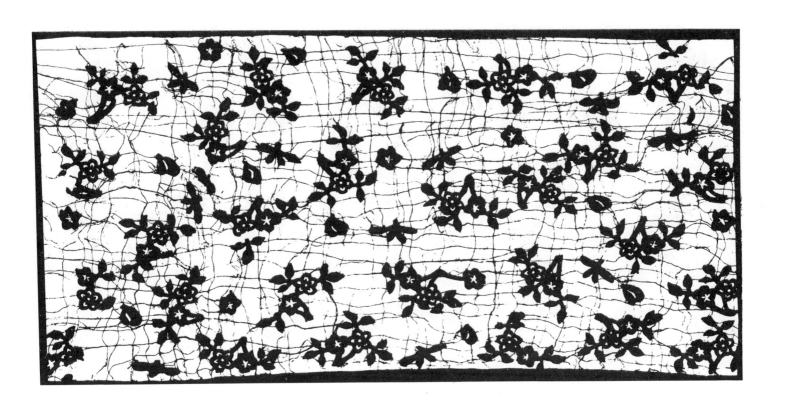

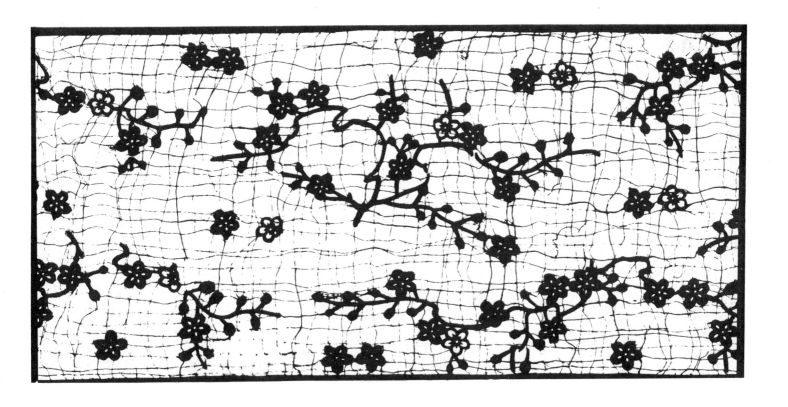

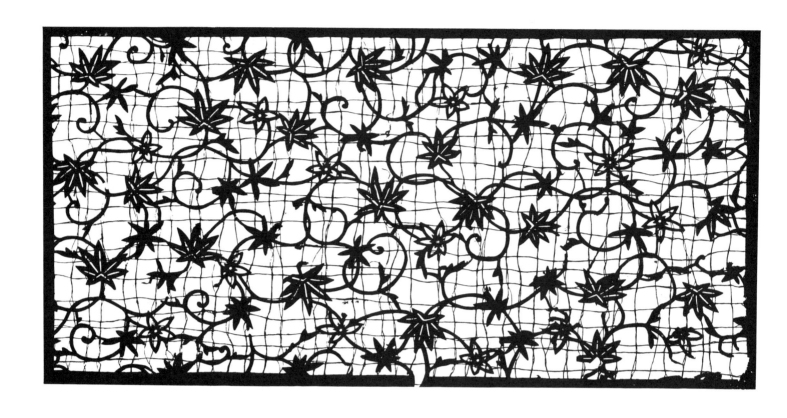

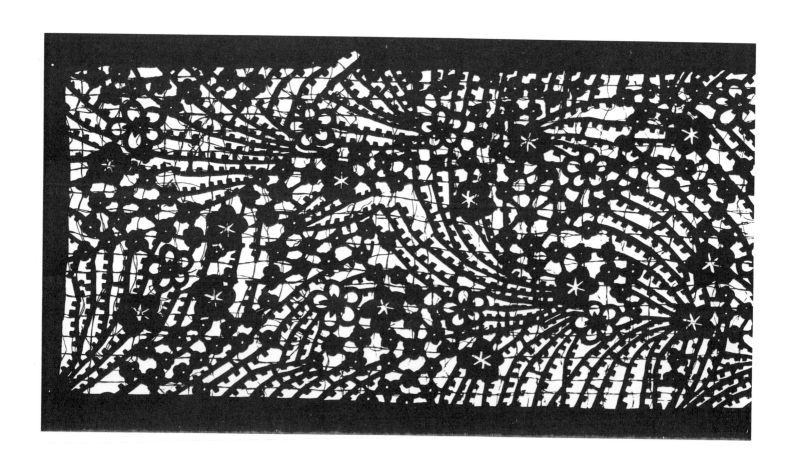

74

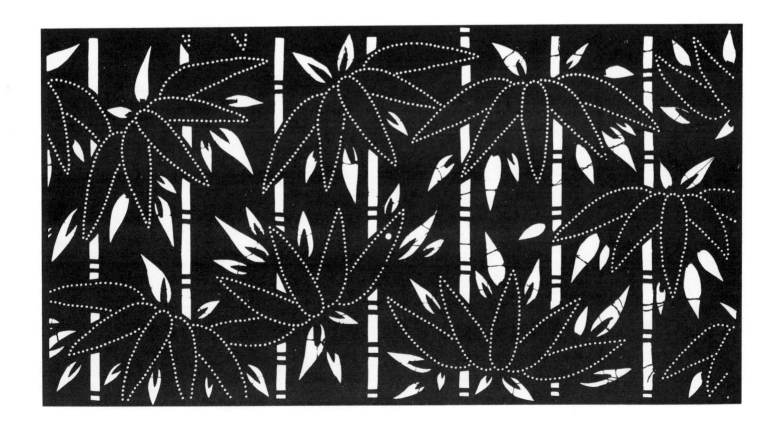

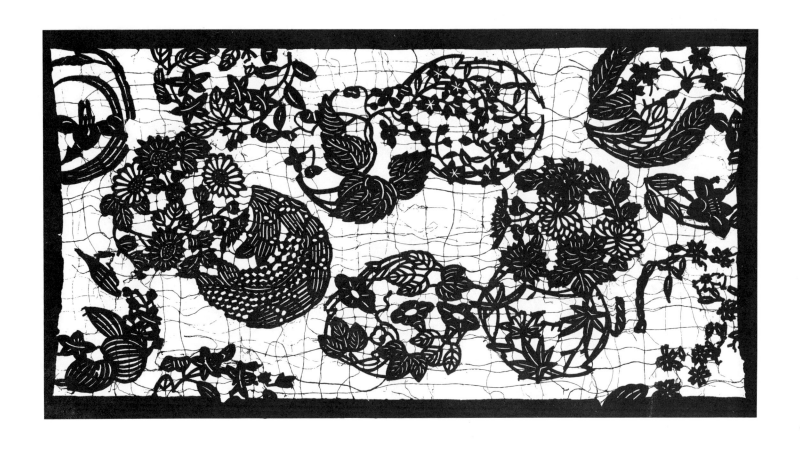

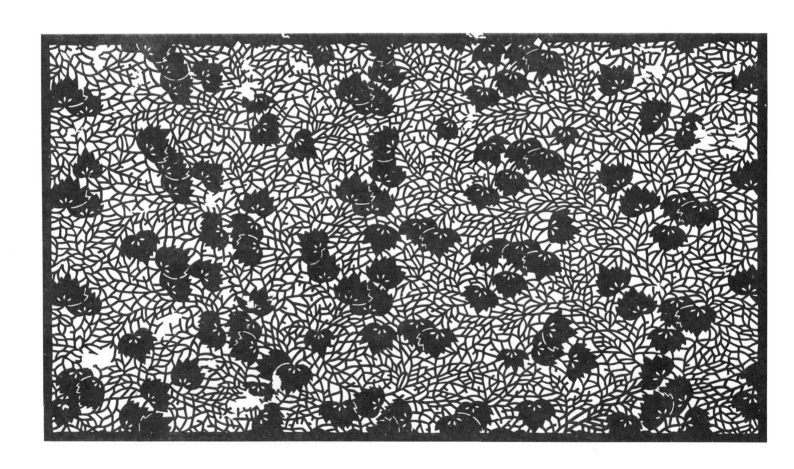

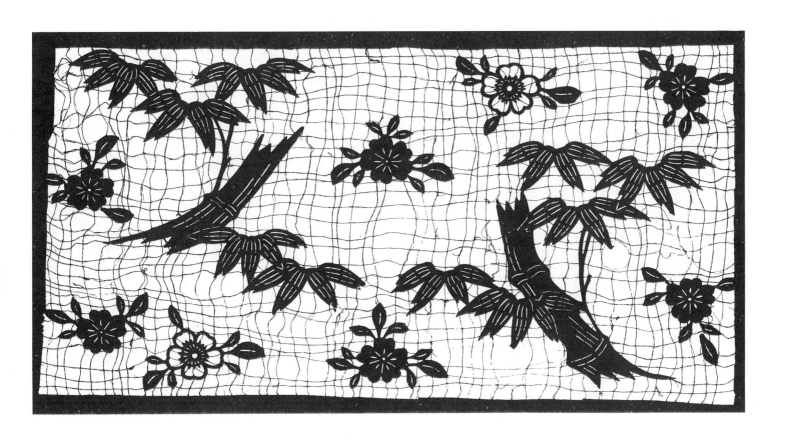

90

94